COMFORT EATING WITH NICK CAVE

VEGAN RECIPES TO GET DEEP INSIDE OF YOU

COMFORT EATING WITH NICK CAVE
Vegan Recipes To Get Deep Inside of You

Cover design by Meggyn Pomerleau
Book design by Joe Biel

First Printing, October 11, 2016

For a catalog, write
Microcosm Publishing
2752 N. Williams Ave
Portland, OR 97227
or visit MicrocosmPublishing.com

ISBN 978-1-62106-613-2
This is Microcosm #259

This is a very serious work of parody. We do not claim to own the work of Nick Cave (though we do love him).

Distributed worldwide by Legato / Perseus and in the UK by Turnaround
This book was printed on post-consumer paper
Global labor conditions are bad, and our roots in industrial Cleveland in the 70s and 80s made us appreciate the need to treat workers right. Therefore, our books are MADE IN THE USA

Library of Congress Cataloging-in-Publication Data
Names: Zingg, Automne. | Ploeg, Joshua.
Title: Comfort Eating with Nick Cave : Vegan Recipes to Get Deep Inside of You / Automne Zingg ; recipes by Joshua Ploeg.
Description: Portland, OR : Microcosm Publishing, 2016.
Identifiers: LCCN 2016000079 | ISBN 9781621066132 (pbk.)
Subjects: LCSH: Vegan cooking--Recipes. | Comfort food--Recipes. | LCGFT: Cookbooks.
Classification: LCC TX837 .Z55 2016 | DDC 641.5/636--dc23
LC record available at http://lccn.loc.gov/2016000079

COMFORT EATING WITH NICK CAVE

VEGAN RECIPES TO GET DEEP INSIDE OF YOU

AUTOMNE ZINGG
RECIPES BY JOSHUA PLOEG

MICROCOSM PUBLISHING
PORTLAND, OR

FRIDGE

Reverse Salt & Pepper Popcorn, 8
Chili, 10
Chocolate Milk, 14
Ice Cream, 16
Frosting, 18
Potato Chips, 20
Onion Rings, 22
Burrito, 26
Tacos, 30
The Face of Jesus in My Soup, 34
Bagel & Cream Cheese, 38
Baked Ziti, 42
Banana Cream Pie, 46
Beef Jerky, 50
Biscuits and Gravy, 52
New York Cheesecake, 56
Chimichanga, 58
Cinnamon Roll, 60
Cookies, 64
Creme Brulee, 66
Mashed Potatoes, 68
French Toast, 70

CONTENTS

Peanut Butter, 72
Grilled Cheez, 74
Mac-n-Cheez for One, 76
Hush Puppies, 78
Deviled Eggs, 80
Funeral Potatoes, 82
Hoagie, 84
Jambalaya, 88
Lamington, 90
Mushy Peas, 94
Pho, 96
Pop Tarte, 100
Ranch Dressing, 102
Ratatouille, 104
Rice Crispy Treats, 108
Reuben, 110
Snackers Bar, 114
Spaghetti and Rice Balls, 118
Stuffed Mushrooms, 120
Tofu Dog, 122
Veggie Meatloaf, 124
Veggie Pot Pie, 126

Introduction

In 2013, I was broke, living in Los Angeles, and going through a terrible breakup. It was probably one of the darkest times in my life and I felt inconsolable. I wasn't working. I wasn't eating. I wasn't drinking. I wasn't doing much of anything except writing depressing songs and listening to even more depressing ones from my youth. I found it curious that the bands that got me through the general malaise of being a sad teenage goth served as a type of sonic comfort food for me as an even sadder adult. Was I having a midlife crisis?

Nick Cave was a particular go-to for me during that time, and he became the musical equivalent to my grandmother's lasagna. I devoured his music and binge listened for months. It was familiar and comforting; I thought whatever feeling emotional eaters gained from consuming a pint of ice cream, I got from blasting "Your Funeral...My Trial." As heartbroken as I was, I reminded myself that Nick Cave had been through much worse. I wondered what he did during those trying times and found myself unconsciously doodling pictures of him weeping while eating. Each day the drawings got a little weirder and my mood got a little better. Eventually, these drawings became a zine, and that zine has now became this cookbook.

Comfort Eating with Nick Cave: Vegan Recipes to Get Deep Inside of You is dedicated to anyone nursing a broken heart, a beer, and a burrito. Come for my illustrations of a weeping Nick Cave shoving funeral potatoes in his mouth. Stay for the incredibly tasty vegan recipes created by the inimitable Joshua Ploeg.

Nom nom nom. Boo hoo hoo.

xoxo,
Automne Zingg

I AM THE BLACK CROW KING
KEEPER OF THE FORGOTTEN
POP
CORN

REVERSE SALT AND PEPPER POPCORN

½ cup popcorn kernels
A few tablespoons of oil (enough to coat bottom of the pan)
An additional tablespoon of coconut oil or margarine, melted
½ teaspoon black salt
¼ teaspoon white pepper

Heat a large pot (make sure it's one with a heavy bottom, a lid, and handles) over medium-high heat with oil to coat the bottom. Add popcorn kernels and shake.

Place lid on top and hold down with potholders as you gently shake the kernels over the flame. It will take several minutes for them to start popping. Whatever you do, don't let hot tears come splashin' on down through the cracks. This makes for soggy popcorn.

Soon there will be a lot of noisy popping going on. Once this dissipates to about a pop every 2 or 3 seconds, remove from heat.

Transfer the popcorn into a bowl, drizzle/shake with melted oil, black salt, and white pepper.

chilli
1st PLACE

CHILI

We found this one printed in an informative six-page feature.

4 cups vegetable broth or tomato/vegetable juice
1 cup shiitake mushrooms, minced
½ cup lentils, uncooked
1 cup black beans, uncooked
1 cup sweet potatoes, diced
¼ cup chipotle peppers, pureed
1 teaspoon cumin
1 ½ teaspoon chili powder
½ teaspoon smoked paprika
1 teaspoon oregano, crumbled
Salt, to taste (soy sauce or tamari if you like)
Pepper, to taste
2 or 3 cloves garlic, minced
1 green bell pepper, diced
1 jalapeño, minced
1 onion, diced
1 cup tomatoes, diced
A few tablespoons cilantro, chopped

Cover black beans in water and soak overnight. Next day, rinse and cover in water again with lentils in a large pot.

Bring to a boil and lower to simmer, adding more water as needed until cooked. Drain the boiling water off, add everything else, and simmer for 30 minutes, adjusting seasonings and liquid level as needed.

If you want to, you can sauté the garlic, onion, bell pepper, and sweet potatoes in a little oil until browned before throwing them in the pot.

BRRRRR

CHOCOLATE
MILK

CHOCOLATE MILK

For cashew-coconut milk:

1 cup raw cashews
3 cups water
1 cup coconut milk
Pinch of salt
1 teaspoon agave or maple syrup
A little vanilla (¼ teaspoon)

For chocolate syrup:

¾ cup water
Pinch of salt
$^{2}/_{3}$ cup cocoa powder (you can use raw for a more reddish color)
$^{2}/_{3}$ cup sugar
Pinch of nutmeg
A little vanilla
2 teaspoons coconut oil

Soak cashews overnight in some water. Discard water, and puree cashews in a powerful blender with 3 cups of water, a pinch salt, and a teaspoon of agave or maple syrup.

Strain through a sieve. Blend in coconut milk and chocolate syrup (below), and serve.

For the syrup, whisk all ingredients except the vanilla together in a saucepan, and stir over medium heat until sugar and chocolate are both melted and incorporated: the sauce simmering and thickened, so sweet and scarlet and free.

Stir in vanilla. Set aside and cool in fridge for a few hours.

ice
cream
Mmmomg
CHOCOLATE CHIP
COOKIE DOUG

ICE CREAM

2 cups coconut milk (including cream)
1 cup pineapple, chopped
1/3 cup brown sugar
1 tablespoon oil
1 teaspoon cornstarch or tapioca flour
1 or 2 pinches salt
2 or 3 tablespoons whiskey

Heat brown sugar with oil, a pinch of salt, and ¼ cup of coconut milk until melted. You may stir occasionally with a wooden spoon. Allow to cool, then blend with other ingredients until smooth.

Place in an ice-cream maker and let 'er rip. Freeze according to your plans.

If you don't have an ice-cream maker, whip it in the blender for 5 minutes or so, then place in a freezer-safe bowl and stir occasionally until frozen like frost from the foothills creeping all around, which will take several hours depending on how cold your shit is.

lick the bowl

FROSTING

½ cup margarine or other hard spread (you can try coconut oil; however, the way it behaves at/above room temperature can cause problems)
2 cups powdered sugar
Pinch of salt
½ teaspoon vanilla
¼ teaspoon lemon extract

I know it's nothing fancy, but you don't drive no Cadillac! Mix all of the ingredients together in a large bowl. Add a little spice if you like. If it's too wet add more powdered sugar. You can add cocoa powder to make it more firm and simultaneously less sweet and more chocolate-y. This will frost a substantial cake.

potato chips
MMMMM
SPICY
FLAVOR

POTATO CHIP

Let's make several because you can't only eat just one!

2 or 3 potatoes
Oil for frying
Salt, to taste
Malt vinegar

For dipping sauce:
1 teaspoon curry powder
1 tablespoon brown or Dijon mustard
1 teaspoon lemon juice
1 tablespoon favorite oil
1 teaspoon truffle oil
¼ cup tofu
¼ teaspoon coriander seeds, crushed
½ teaspoon dill, chopped
Salt and pepper, to taste
A little broth or water to help with the texture

Dipping sauce is easy, just blend it all on high until smooth; adjust seasoning and liquid as needed.

Slice potatoes thinly, and salt. Place on paper towels, cover with more towels, and press with a pan while you heat the oil to a frying temperature (375 is good; 350 is fine). Fry the potatoes in batches until crispy, then set on absorbent paper and shake with salt.

Sprinkle a little malt vinegar on before serving.

onion
rings

ONION RINGS

These are addictive and you'll want to remember this, so tear out the page and stuff it inside your shirt.

2 onions

1 ¼ cup beer

¾ cup flour

½ cup rice flour

1 teaspoon baking powder or soda

¾ teaspoon salt

Oil for frying, plus 2 tablespoons

1 teaspoon garlic powder

½ teaspoon turmeric

2 tablespoons nutritional yeast (or something else equally delicious)

¼ teaspoon white or black pepper

2 tablespoons potato starch

1 teaspoon sugar

Cut the ends off of the onions, then peel and slice them into rings. Set in a bowl with ¼ cup beer, ¼ teaspoon each of the salt and the pepper. Meanwhile, blend the other ingredients together except the frying oil (dry ingredients first, then add wet) in a large mixing bowl. Add liquid if needed, and adjust seasonings to taste. Should be the consistency of pancake batter.

Heat your oil to 350 degrees (or a little hotter). Dredge the onion rings in batter until coated and fry in batches until browned. Drain on absorbent paper. If you do this in a pan rather than a fryer, you can brown them on one side and then carefully flip them.

Make sure to eat these with some barbecue sauce or other flavorful addition for in your heart it will never be spring if you eat that plain gold ring. Just trust me.

I DO

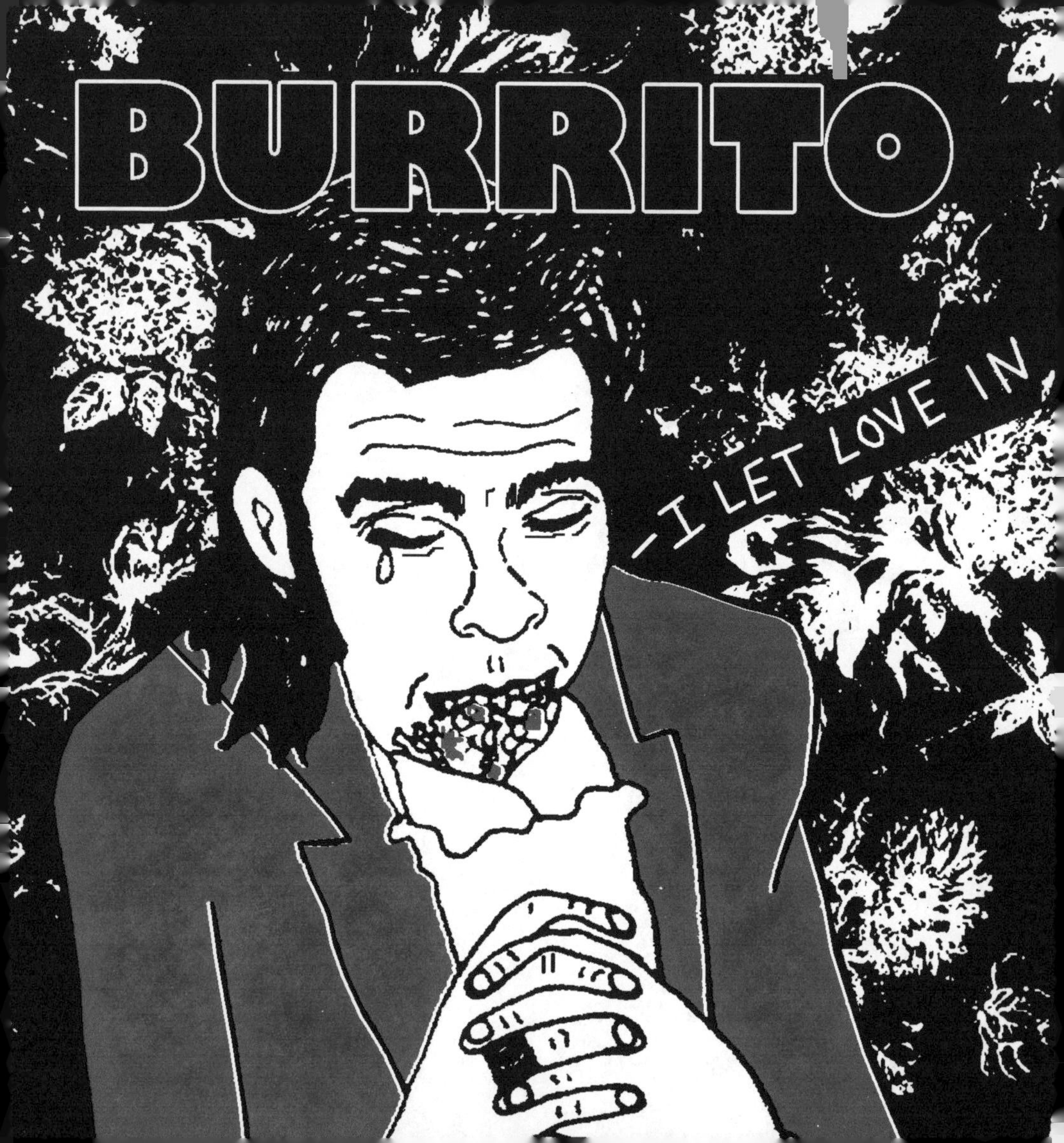
BURRITO
—I LET LOVE IN

BURRITO

You will need some rather large tortillas

For jalapeño salsa fresca:

2 jalapeños, seeded and minced *(scorch them in fire first for a nice touch!)*
Juice of 1 lime
Chili powder, salt, pepper, and coriander, to taste
2 garlic cloves, minced
1 cup tomatoes, diced
½ cup onion, minced
¼ cup cilantro, chopped

For peruano beans:

1 cup canary beans
1 or 2 chipotle peppers
1 onion, diced
2 garlic cloves
2 sage leaves, chopped
Salt, as needed
A little liquid smoke or smoky salt
2 or 3 tablespoons oil

For seasoned rice:

1 cup rice

Water or broth, to cover

1 tomato, diced

½ cup onion, minced

½ cup red and green bell pepper, minced

Salt or seasoning blend, to taste

½ teaspoon each cumin and chili powder

For Anaheim potatoes:

1 cup potatoes, diced

2 Anaheim peppers, diced

Chili powder, oregano, and cumin, to taste

1 clove garlic, minced

¼ cup onion, minced

2 or 3 tablespoons oil

Soak the beans/peruanos overnight, then drain, bring to a boil with all but salt in a pot with water aplenty. Once cooked, drain some of the water out, and then salt and mash them, or just leave them whole.

Cook your rice with all ingredients and water to cover (up to first knuckle, or other appropriate method).

While that is going on, fry up those potatoes in oil, adding a little water, and cover for 10 minutes over medium heat in a large skillet. Turn at least once in this time and re-cover. After your 10 minutes are up, add the rest and keep frying until taters are soft and peppers are yummy.

Mix together the ingredients for the salsa, set aside. Wear gloves for the jalapeño if you must, but remember it's wise to lay down your gloves and just give in.

Warm your tortillas over flame or in a pan, turning until they are good and ready. (This helps them to not break or get pasty, and also, technically, to be completely cooked; it only takes a very short time per side, so don't burn them! You can also do this in an oven if you have to).

Put some of everything in your damn tortilla and roll it, son!

TACOS
ONE MORE

TACOS

10 corn tortillas
Salt, to taste
2 cups cactus, cut into strips (and uh, without needles)
Chili powder and cumin
Oil

For tomatillo salsa:

1 cup, tomatillos, peeled and chopped
½ teaspoon each coriander, cumin, chili powder, and white pepper
½ cup onion, minced
1 tablespoon jalapeño, minced
2 cloves garlic, minced
1 tablespoon oil

For pico de gallo with red cabbage:

1 cup red cabbage
1 jalapeño, minced
2 tablespoons cilantro, minced
1 cup tomato, diced
2 garlic cloves, minced
½ cup white onion, minced
Juice of 1 lime

For refried black beans:

1 ½ cups cooked black beans

3 or 4 tablespoons oil (coconut's great)

½ teaspoon chili powder

2 tablespoons onion, minced or grated

1 garlic clove, minced

2 or 3 tablespoons veggie bacon, minced

Vegetable broth as needed (only a couple tablespoons)

Place all of the tomatillo salsa ingredients in a saucepan and cook, stirring for 5 minutes. Remove from heat. Cool and puree (unless you want a chunky texture), adding salt to taste. Set aside.

Mix cabbage/pico ingredients together with a little salt and set aside, and adjust seasonings to taste or add spices.

Cook onions, garlic, and bacon in oil for refried beans for 2 minutes. Add black beans and mash with chili powder and a little broth. Stir. When it bubbles and starts to crisp around the edge of the pan, it's done. Or whenever you say it's done, it's done.

Sauté cactus in a little oil with chili powder and cumin and a little salt until browned. Set aside.

You will want to heat each tortilla over flame on both sides until warm and maybe with a couple of marks to show for it.

Fill tortillas with a bit of each item until stuffed full of incubus, or chocka block with succubus.

Serve with lime and cilantro.

the face of Jesus in my
soup

SOUP GOLDEN HARVEST SOUP WITH CRANBERRY RELISH

4 cups veggie broth (more as needed)
1 ½ teaspoons turmeric
A few saffron threads
Salt, to taste
A little sage, dried and crumbled
1 tablespoon oil
2 cups sweet potatoes, chopped
2 cups rutabagas or turnips, diced
1 cup golden beets, diced
1 cup parsley root (or parsnip), chopped
¼ cup burdock root, peeled and minced
½ cup onion, diced
2 garlic cloves, minced
½ cup carrot, diced
A little lemon juice

Begin by sautéing the vegetables and garlic in oil in a nice soup pot with a little salt. After 3 minutes, add sage, turmeric, and saffron, and then stir. When you smell a fancy fragrance, add the broth and the rest (haha, just add all of that after 1 minute). Bring to simmer and cook, adding more liquid as necessary for 25 to 40 minutes (depending on how soft you like your roots to be, just let simmer until behind the locked gates an old donkey moans). Adjust seasoning to taste.

For cranberry relish:

Cook 1 cup cranberries in ½ cup pomegranate juice with salt and pepper to taste, ¼ cup chopped red onion, a little carrot and ginger, ½ teaspoon garam masala, a little sugar to taste, 2 teaspoons of oil, 1 tablespoon chopped parsley, a little lemon juice, and a pinch each of cloves, cardamom, and curry powder. You can also add red or orange bell pepper, orange, chilies, or what have you. When the cranberries are cooked, give the whole thing a quick coarse blend and adjust seasonings to taste. It won't take long, about 10 minutes.

—sinfully delicious

BAGEL & CREAM CHEESE

BAGEL WITH CREAM CHEESE

For bagel:

3 cups flour

1 package dry active yeast

1 cup warm water

¼ or ½ teaspoon salt

2 teaspoons sugar

1 tablespoon oil

For cream cheese:

1 cup tofu or cooked white bean

½ cup cashew, soy, or other milk

½ teaspoon sugar (or 1 teaspoon agave)

1 teaspoon agar flakes or carrageenan

¼ teaspoon mustard powder

Oil

1 clove garlic, peeled

2 teaspoons cider vinegar

½ teaspoon salt (more or less to taste)

¼ cup oil

Puree ingredients for cream cheese except cider vinegar. Cook over low-medium heat in a saucepan, stirring with a wooden spoon or rubber spatula until thick. Remove from heat and stir in vinegar. Allow to cool. Season more to taste and place in a tub in the fridge.

Activate yeast with sugar in warm water in a bowl. Add in flour and salt, using more if needed, to make a workable dough. Form into a flat ball and coat with oil. Cover and let stand for 2 hours.

Roll onto a lightly oiled board and cut into 12 strips. Form into rings. Allow to rise again for 15 minutes—don't worry, she'll be rising by the time you get to Phoenix.

Bring several cups of water to boil in a pot. You can add some agave to this if you'd like. Boil bagels 3 or 4 at a time, turning once for about a minute or so. Set aside and drain off excess water. Place on a parchment-lined baking sheet and bake them at 450 degrees for about 15 minutes.

MMMPH
LOX

BAKED ZITI

FEELS GOOD
INSIDE OF ME.

BAKED ZITI

3 cups ziti, cooked al dente
2 ½ cup crushed tomatoes
Salt and pepper, to taste
½ teaspoon balsamic vinegar
1 cup garbanzo or white beans, cooked and smashed
1 cup onion, chopped
4 garlic cloves, minced
¼ cup basil, chopped
1 cup olives, sliced
1 cup red bell peppers, diced
1 cup spinach, chopped
1 cup mushrooms, chopped
2 tablespoons olive oil

For cheezy sauce:
1 tablespoon prepared brown mustard
1 tablespoon white miso
½ cup artichoke hearts
3 garlic cloves, peeled
1 tablespoon cider vinegar or white wine vinegar
1 cup tofu or cooked white beans
¼ cup flour, potato starch, or rice flour

¼ cup oil or margarine (or whatever)
1 cup broth or cashew (or other) milk
Salt and white pepper, to taste
(You may also add nutritional yeast if you like)

Mix all ingredients except those for cheezy sauce, and dump in a lightly greased 9 inch x 13 inch pan like night, the shameless widow, doffed her leaves in a pile. Cover with foil and bake at 375 degrees for 35 minutes.

Blend all ingredients for cheezy sauce and adjust seasonings to taste. Set aside.

Remove ziti from oven, take off foil, and raise temp to 425. Coat top with cheezy sauce. Return to oven and bake an additional 15 to 20 minutes. You can also broil the top if you like.

banana
cream
pie

BANANA CREAM PIE

3 cups sliced bananas
¼ to ½ cup quinoa flour (or ½ cup tofu + 2 tablespoons cornstarch)
¾ cup sugar
¼ cup powdered sugar
1 cup coconut milk
1 cup coconut cream
1 teaspoon vanilla
1 teaspoon lemon juice
1 ¼ cup flour
½ cup margarine/oil/coconut oil + several tablespoons water as needed (a few tablespoons)
Salt, to taste

Crumb together flour, ½ cup margarine, a little salt, and a few tablespoons of water to make a workable dough for crust. Cover and set aside.

Puree quinoa flour, coconut milk, 1 cup of the bananas, half of the vanilla, half of the lemon juice, a tablespoon or two of oil, pinch of salt, and ½ cup sugar. Heat over medium-low in a saucepan until thickened, adjusting seasonings to taste. Use as much quinoa flour as needed. Set aside to cool.

Blend coconut cream, powdered sugar, rest of lemon juice, and vanilla and place in fridge.

Roll out pie crust to fit a greased 9-inch pie pan on a floured board. Bake at 425 degrees for 10 minutes, then lower to 375 and bake until lightly browned (about 12 to 15 minutes).

Pour quinoa/banana mixture into pie crust, alternating with sliced bananas sprinkled with sugar. Chill (it should become relatively firm). You can also freeze it, and then thaw it out to serve.

Spread coconut cream mixture on top and chill again in the fridge. If someone tries to open it, let them know there's a woman-pie in there and you're the best cook they've ever had.

EVERYTHING
IS FINE

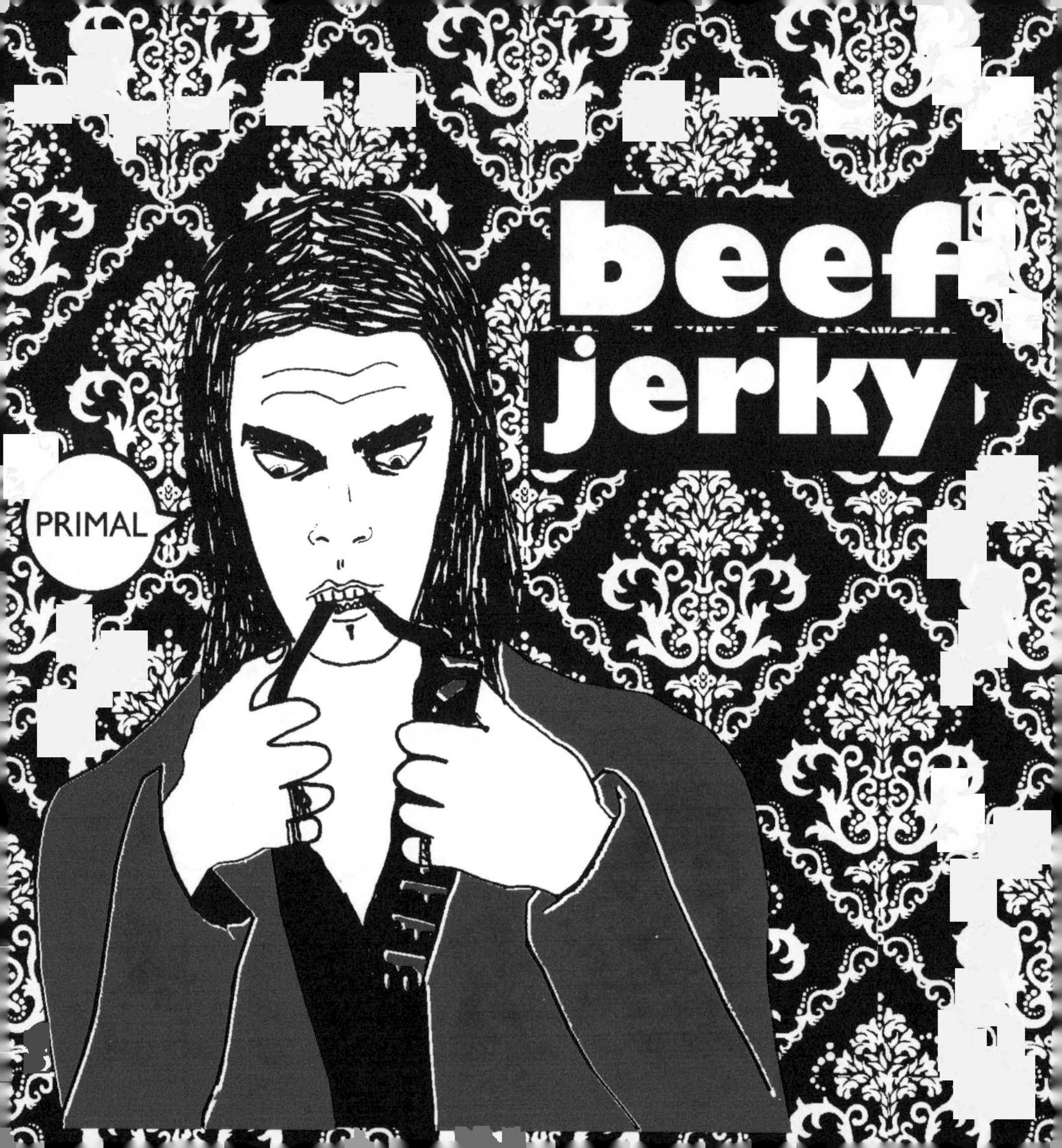
beef
jerky
PRIMAL

"BEEF" JERKY

2 pounds tofu, eggplant, or portabella, thinly sliced
½ cup tamari or teriyaki
2 tablespoons vegan Worcestershire
2 or 3 tablespoons agave
1 tablespoon oil
2 teaspoons black pepper
½ teaspoon liquid smoke
1 tablespoon tomato paste

Blend tamari, oil, agave, Worcestershire, black pepper, liquid smoke, and tomato paste.

Soak tofu in marinade for a few hours. Drain. Place tofu on a baking sheet and cook 4 hours at 250, or overnight in a dehydrator (at 115 degrees or so; it may take longer), turning every now and again. If you like, part way through, you can baste the tofu with the marinade again and continue on, probably toward the end/later half when the scaffold is high and eternity is near.

biscuits
and
gravy
BURY MY
FEELINGS.

BISCUITS & GRAVY

For biscuit:

1 ½ cup flour

2 teaspoons baking powder

½ teaspoon cream of tartar

1/3 cup oil/shortening

1/3 cup soy or cashew milk (more or less as needed)

1 teaspoon salt

½ cup onion, grated

¼ cup parsley, chopped

For gravy:

1 cup mushrooms, chopped

1 ½ cups mushroom broth (can add some "milk" if you like, too)

1 tablespoon tamari

½ teaspoon cumin

¼ teaspoon black pepper

Salt, to taste

1 teaspoon oregano, crushed

¼ teaspoon liquid smoke

1 cup onion, diced

2 or 3 garlic cloves, minced

½ cup seasoned tempeh, crumbled

2 tablespoons flour
¼ cup margarine or oil + 1 tablespoon

Not another biscuits and gravy recipe, you say? Well, whoa whoa whoa, you must be the prophet because you know everything I've done!

Combine all dry ingredients for biscuit. Cut in oil/shortening to make crumbs. Add onion and parsley. Add in "milk," combining to make a soft dough. Roll out onto lightly floured board to ½ inch thick and cut into squares or rounds. Bake on lightly greased sheet (or parchment covered) at 450 degrees for 12 to 15 minutes.

Sauté tempeh with tamari in 1 tablespoon oil, adding garlic and onion, until browned. Set aside.

Heat margarine in a saucepan, whisk in flour. When it begins to thicken, add in broth. Add mushrooms, smoke, and the rest, and cook for about 5 minutes. Add in tempeh mixture and cook for another 5 minutes, adjusting seasonings to taste. If it's too thick, whisk in more liquid derp.

BURY MY FEELINGS.

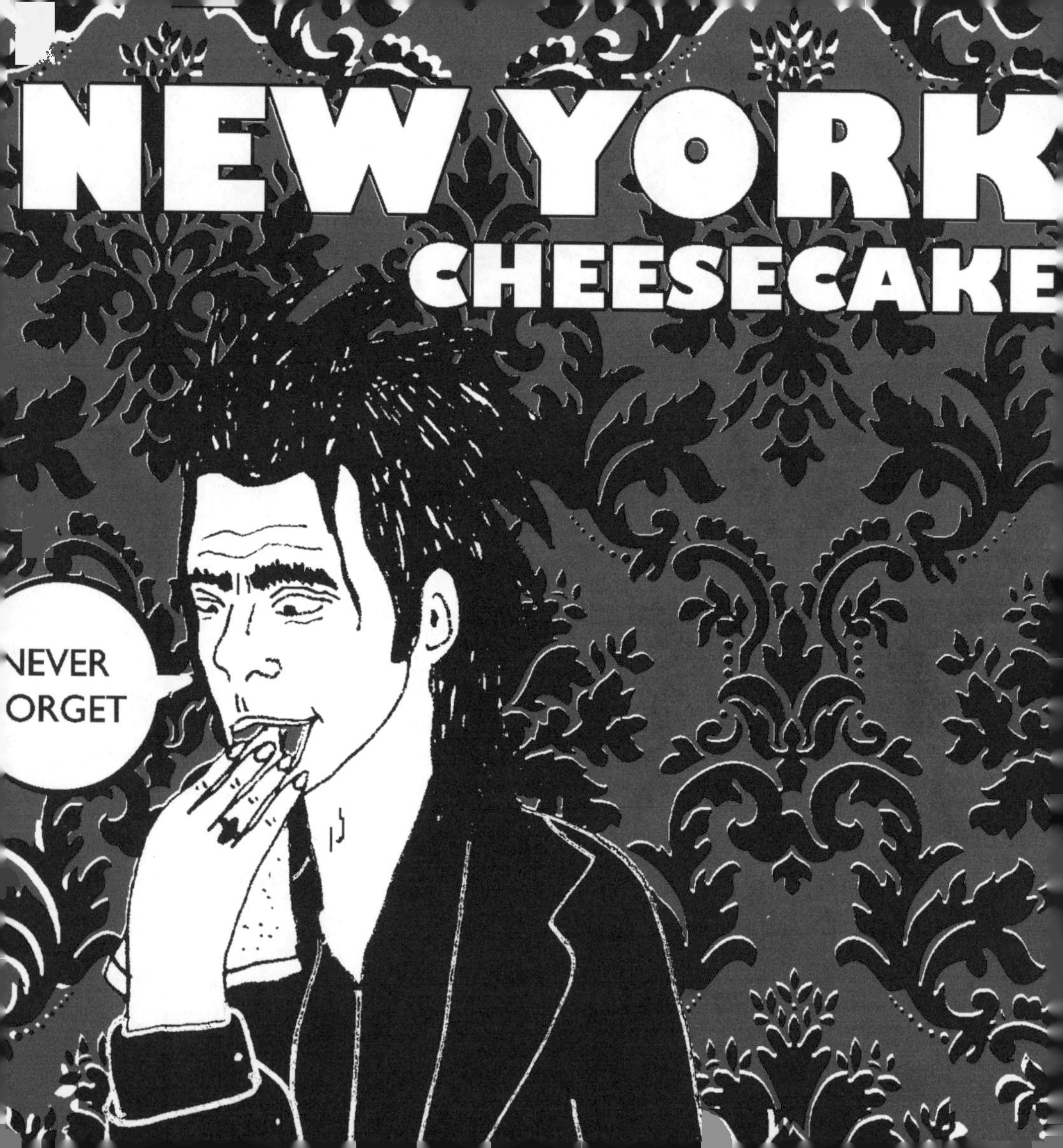
NEW YORK
CHEESECAKE
NEVER
ORGET

CHEESECAKE

1 ½cup tofu
1 ½ cups coconut cream
2 teaspoons agar flakes
2 tablespoons cornstarch
½ cup rice or sorgum flour
½ teaspoon baking powder
1 tablespoon cider vinegar or lemon juice
¼ teaspoon mustard powder
½ teaspoon salt (more or less to taste)
2 tablespoons nutritional yeast
½ cup sugar
1 teaspoon lemon zest
1 teaspoon vanilla
1 ½ cup almonds, ground
⅓ cup brown sugar
½ cup coconut oil/ margarine + a couple extra tablespoons

Mix together almonds, brown sugar, and ½ cup coconut oil. Press into the bottom of a 9-inch pie pan, spring form pan, or a bottle and a box and a cradle of straw.

Blend the other ingredients, adjusting flavors a bit to taste. Pour into pie crust and bake at 375 degrees for 40 minutes. Allow to cool, then chill.

chimichanga
GET
IN
THERE

CHIMICHANGA

6 large tortillas (large is 16 inches or bigger, btw)
2 cups veg-beef, shiitake, or tempeh
2 tablespoons tamari
1 ½ tablespoons tomato paste
1 cup onion, diced
3 or 4 garlic cloves, minced
A few tablespoon oil (plus oil for deep frying)
1 ½ teaspoons chili powder
1 teaspoon ground cumin
1 teaspoon oregano, crushed
½ cup cabbage, shredded
1 jalapeño, minced
¼ cup chopped cilantro
½ cup favorite uncheeze
⅓ cup favorite salsa
Hot sauce

Sauté onions, jalapeños, and garlic in a couple tablespoons oil for 3 minutes. Add veg-beef. Stir, and add oregano and spices, tomato paste, and tamari, plus a little hot sauce. Cook until "beef" is browned. Set aside.

Place a scoop of this on each tortilla with cabbage, uncheeze, salsa, and cilantro. Roll these up rill tight. Fry in deep oil, turning once, until lightly browned and crispy everywhere.

These are especially great if your heart and soul are kind of famished.

cinnamon roll
EROTIC BUNS

CINNAMON ROLL

4 cups flour (more or less as needed)

1 package active dry yeast

1 cup soy, almond, or cashew milk

¼ cup sugar

1 teaspoon vanilla

1 teaspoon salt

2 teaspoons baking powder

½ cup crushed pecans

½ cup golden raisins

⅓ cup softened margarine or coconut oil

½ cup packed brown sugar

2 ½ teaspoons ground cinnamon

For glaze:

½ cup margarine or coconut oil

½ cup brown sugar

¼ cup powdered sugar

A little flour (about 1 tablespoon)

½ cup pecans, crushed

¼ teaspoon salt

½ teaspoon extra cinnamon

In a large bowl, combine a cup of the flour with yeast. Warm the soy milk with sugar, sugar sugar, O sugar it's a drag, margarine, and salt til warm. Add to the flour mixture. Add the rest of the flour, baking powder, vanilla, and salt with as much flour or liquid as needed to make a soft but workable dough (not overly sticky for this one).

Form dough into a ball, grease lightly, and place in a bowl covered to rise for an hour and a half. Separate dough into halves. Roll half out on a lightly floured surface to about 12-inch x 8- or 9-inch size.

Spread with half of the softened margarine and sprinkle with half the cinnamon and brown sugar, raisins, and nuts. Roll this up (so that it's 12 inches long, you roll it the shorter way). Seal the edges and repeat with the other half.

Slice each roll into 6 pieces. Place in greased 9-inch x 13-inch pan with the cut side down, and allow to rise for another hour. Sprinkle with remaining cinnamon.

Bake at 350 degrees for 25 to 30 minutes or until browned. You can mix the glaze ingredients together and pour over the top for the last 5 to 10 minutes of baking, or after the rolls are done.

cookies.
MMMmmmmm
SOOTHING.

COOKIES

Double Nut Nut Double Butter Chocolate Chip in this case

3 cups flour
½ cup sugar
½ cup brown sugar
½ cup chocolate chips
½ cup peanut butter
¼ cup cashew butter
½ cup roasted cashews
½ cup roasted peanuts
1 teaspoon vanilla
2 teaspoons baking powder
½ teaspoon salt
2 tablespoons cornstarch or potato starch
¼ cup cashew milk
½ cup margarine, shortening or coconut oil

Mix flour, salt, starch, and baking powder in a mixing bowl and set aside. Separately mix all of the wet ingredients (including margarine and nut butters). Add in sugars as well.

Add in batches to the flour mixture, followed by nuts and chocolate chips to make a nice yummy cookie dough. Check it—it might need a little extra salt or something.

Roll out into a log about 1 ½ inches thick. Cut into 24 rounds. Place them on parchment on a cookie sheet and bake at 350 degrees for about 12 minutes or until browned, being careful not to overcook and wind up with bricks of grief and stricken mortar.

Set aside cookies to cool on a rack soon after they come out.

I LOVE YOU
creme
brulee

CREME BRULEE

1 cup coconut puree
1 cup tofu
½ teaspoon lemon juice
½ teaspoon orange zest
½ cup sugar + ¼ cup more sugar
1 tablespoon cornstarch or other starch
¼ cup flour or sorghum flour (or other not-gross-tasting flour)
1 teaspoon vanilla
¼ cup oil/coconut oil or margarine
¼ teaspoon salt *(more to taste, may be done half with black salt for a more farty egg taste, since this here is a dish that normally uses a lot of egg yolks)*

Blend all but extra sugar and pour into 4 to 6 ramekins. Bake at 350 degrees for 30 minutes (you can place the ramekins in a baking pan with a little water, if you like).

Remove and cool for a bit. Sprinkle each with about a tablespoon of sugar, then broil for 2 to 3 minutes, or run over the top with a torch to make the burnt sugar crack on top, which will leadeth you like a lamb to the lips.

mashed potatoes
OHH

MASHED POTATOES

2 pounds of potatoes
Salt and pepper, to taste
3 or 4 tablespoons oil or margarine
1 teaspoon garlic powder
2 tablespoons chives, minced
2 tablespoons parsley, minced
Favorite vegan milk, as needed (unsweetened)

Scrub potatoes and poke with a fork. Boil whole in water to cover for around 20 minutes, or until cooked through. Drain most of the water out, reserving 1/3 to ½ cup of the liquid. Mash together with salt, pepper, and oil (add more liquid if needed), and then stir in garlic powder, parsley, and chives until both smooth and lumpy like a snowman with six holes clean into his fat fucking guts.

For fun, use ranch dressing (page 102) as the liquid for this. These potatoes are also great with chopped up green olives, peperoncini, and capers.

french
toast
OUI

FRENCH TOAST

4 slices stale or toasted toast

For batter:

½ cup tofu
¼ cup coconut oil
¼ cup nutritional yeast
⅓ cup flour
Salt, to taste
2 or 3 tablespoons sugar
½ teaspoon baking powder or soda
¼ teaspoon cinnamon
A pinch or two nutmeg
½ teaspoon vanilla
1 cup liquid such as vanilla soy milk, almond milk, or whatever

Blend the batter ingredients until smooth. Adjust flavors to taste. Add more liquid if need be. Soak bread slices in this until well coated. Fry in light oil in a pan, turning once, until browned.

Serve with jam, syrup, or whatever. Or how about marmalade, vegan sour cream, or powdered sugar? (Your eyes'll be like wheels spinnin' round and round, jerkin'-off at every sound.) Or mix peanut butter with your favorite vegan milk and powdered sugar, and have it with that and maple syrup—that's also good.

butter
OHH MY GOD
EXTRA CRUNCH

PEANUT BUTTER

1 cup peanuts, shelled and roasted

1 cup hazelnuts or cashews, peeled (roasted is fine: Why? Because you can!)

2 tablespoons peanut oil (more as needed)

Salt, to taste

Add a little agave, if you like

Turmeric is also nice in this

Mix these things together, then blend in a food processor until smooth. Your chain of command has been silenced now: it's ready! Adjust seasoning to taste.

IN-N-OUT GRILLED CHEESE
MMMMM ANIMAL STYLE
IN-N-OUT

GRILLED CHEEZ

1 or 2 cloves garlic, peeled

2 or 3 tablespoons miso

½ cup potato or cashews, cooked and peeled

¼ cup broth (more if needed)

1 teaspoon mustard

1 ½ teaspoon cider vinegar

¼ cup nutritional yeast *(if you are sick of nutritional yeast, just use a couple tablespoons alternative flour and some garlic powder; maybe, a few slices of red bell pepper)*

1 tablespoon oil + some for frying

Salt and white pepper, to taste

4 slices favorite bread

Blend all but the bread until smooth. Heat this concoction for a few minutes, stirring over med-low heat until it starts to bubble, and then season to taste. Allow to cool.

Use to make sandwiches with the bread. Fry in light oil, turning once, until the shiv is golden the shiv is golden the shiv is golden, on both sides. Tomato slices, sautéed mushrooms, or pickles can be added.

I START TO CRY
I START TO CRY

MAC N CHEEZ

Cook pasta to make 2 cups, cooked and drained (you will be cooking it for 1 to 2 minutes more in the sauce so pretty al dente is good)

For sauce:
¼ cup sauerkraut
⅓ cup cashews
2 tablespoons miso
1 tablespoon prepared mustard
Salt and white pepper, to taste
¼ cup onion, diced
2 tablespoons lemon juice (or more)
A splash of white balsamic, red wine vinegar, or cider vinegar
1 cup mushroom broth (more or less depending on thickness you want)
¼ cup tahini
2 or 3 garlic cloves
2 tablespoons tapioca or potato starch (use more if needed)
½ teaspoon turmeric
Salt and pepper, to taste

This is comforting...if you're on a real low-down bummer, stare deep into the abyss and say 'this one is for mama,' and you're sure to feel better.

Blend sauce ingredients together, and season to taste. Cook in a saucepan over medium heat for 3 to 5 minutes, adding more liquid (maybe beer) as needed to keep it nice and saucy. Mix in pasta, cook for a minute or two more, adjusting seasoning to taste.

HUSH
PUPPIES
SHHHHH

HUSH PUPPIES

1 cup corn meal
1 teaspoon baking powder
Salt, to taste
½ teaspoon chili powder
¼ cup flour or alt. flour
2 or 3 tablespoons oil + some for frying
½ teaspoon onion or onion powder
About ½ cup warm water

Mix these together, add more water if need be, and season to taste. Should make a batter that's thicker than pancake batter, but not quite as hard as biscuit dough.

Drop batter by the tablespoon full into hot oil and fry, hush-a-bye don't you cry, go to sleep my little babies, turning until browned and tasty.

up jumped the
DEVILED
EGGS
UNHOLY
GOODNESS

DEVILLED EGG

16-ounce block extra firm tofu, cut in half along the width (like, to maximize surface area)
A little oil
Salt, black salt, and white pepper, to taste
1 tablespoon mustard
½ teaspoon turmeric
½ cup cooked garbanzo beans
½ teaspoon lemon juice
1 tablespoon onion, chopped
1 tablespoon nutritional yeast
Paprika, for sprinkling
Parsley sprigs

Cut tofu into 12 squares. Sauté lightly in a little oil with some salt and white pepper, and then set aside to cool off. With a teaspoon, scoop out a little indentation in the top of each square. Place these extra scoops of tofu with mustard, lemon juice, garbanzos, black salt, a little white pepper, lemon juice, turmeric, nutritional yeast, onion, and about 2 teaspoons of oil in a food processor, and blend to whatever texture you like. Adjust seasonings to taste.

Fill the tofu squares with this mixture, sprinkle with paprika, and place parsley sprigs on top.

Make it look pretty just like Martha Stewart would—must I kill that woman? Must I kill that woman?

Chill and serve.

R.I.P.
IN MY
TUMMY
your
FUNERAL
my trial
POTATOES

FUNERAL POTATOES

I've eaten nearly a whole tray of these once at a church potluck back in the day. It was great! They were all aghast; I could see their frightened faces peering at me through the gate.

4 cups potatoes, cooked and diced
1 cup your favorite vegan "sour cream"
1 onion, diced
3 garlic cloves, minced
2 tablespoons parsley, minced
1 ½ cup corn flakes
1 cup margarine or coconut oil
1 cup of your favorite vegan cheez, shredded
White pepper and salt, to taste
¼ cup flour or rice flour
½ cup broth
¼ cup nutritional yeast

Mix potatoes, "sour cream," onion, flour, parsley, broth, garlic, salt and pepper to taste, as well as half of the cheez, half of the oil, and half of the nutritional yeast. Pour this into an 8-inch x 11-inch baking dish.

Crumb together cornflakes with rest of oil and cheez, nutritional yeast, and salt and pepper to taste, if needed. Sprinkle on top of the potato dish. Bake at 375 degrees for 30 minutes.

hoagie

HOAGIE CANNELLINI MEATBALL SANDWICH

4 hoagie rolls
Arugula, to garnish
Tomatoes, sliced
1 onion, sliced
1 green or red bell pepper, sliced
½ cup marinara sauce
¼ cup olives, chopped

For balls:

1 cup cannellini beans, cooked
½ cup sunflower seeds, roasted
Salt and pepper, to taste
¼ cup onion, diced
1 tablespoon oil
¼ cup parsley
¼ cup flour or quinoa flour (more as needed)

For pesto mayo:

½ cup basil
1 tablespoon oregano
3 or 4 garlic cloves
2 or 3 tablespoons olive oil

1 tablespoon lemon juice (more to taste)
2 tablespoons tofu, cooked white beans, or raw cashews
A little broth or water, as needed
Salt, to taste

Sauté onions and peppers in a little oil with salt and pepper until cooked to your liking.

Coarsely blend cannelini beans, sunflower seeds, onion, and parsley. Mix with flour, a tablespoon of oil, salt, and pepper. Form into balls and fry in light oil, turning until browned. Set aside.

Blend ingredients for pesto mayo, adding liquid if needed, and adjusting seasonings.

Split and toast your rolls. Spread pesto on top and bottom, followed by balls and olives, marinara, then sautéed onions and peppers, then tomato slices and arugula. Peperoncini can also make a nice addition, or pickles. You could say that God invented this amazing sandwich but I'm afraid that God lives only in our dreams. So it seems.

G

HOLD ME
jambalaya

JAMBALAYA

1 cup sweet potato, diced
2 cups eggplant, tempeh, or mushrooms (or a combo!!)
1 onion, diced
4 garlic cloves, minced
1 cup okra, sliced
1 cup tomato sauce
1 cup broth
2 tablespoons chile or chipotle sauce
1 cup red and green bell peppers, diced
1 ½ teaspoon smoked paprika
1 cup red beans, cooked
1 ½ cup cooked brown rice
1 ½ teaspoons oregano or file
A couple tablespoons tamarind, HP, Worcestershire, or other sauce
Salt and pepper, to taste
A few tablespoons of oil

Sauté half of the onion and garlic in some oil. Add sweet potato and cook with the lid on for 5 minutes. Add eggplant, etc. Cook for 5 more minutes. Add half the peppers, half the tomato sauce, okra, broth, ⅔ of the seasonings, salt and pepper to taste, and cook for another 15 minutes, adjusting seasonings as needed.

Meanwhile fry up the rest of the onion, peppers, and garlic in a little oil with some salt. Add rice, stir in rest of tomato sauce, red beans, spices, and everything until you've emptied out the peopled halls, nailed shut the windows and locked the doors and cook for 5 minutes or so, stirring.

Serve together.

lamington

LAMINGTON

2 cups flour
¾ cup sugar
3 teaspoons baking powder
1 tablespoon cornstarch or 1 teaspoon ground flax seeds with 1 tablespoon water
¼ cup oil
1 teaspoon vanilla
1 ¼ cups water or favorite milk
A pinch of salt

This is a great traditional piece of cake. Normally, it's best to leave these ancient places to the angels: Let the saints attend to their keeping of the cathedrals, but in this case, it's worth the risk to enjoy a tasty morsel.

Mix dry ingredients in a mixing bowl. Add the wet ingredients and mix.

Grease a square 8-inch x 8-inch cake pan and flour it lightly. Pour in batter and bake at 350 degrees for 30 to 40 minutes, or until toothpick comes out clean.

Allow to cool briefly then turn out onto a wire rack. Cut into 2-inch squares.

Combine:

1 ½ cups powdered sugar

$^1/_3$ cup of cocoa powder

2 tablespoons margarine or coconut oil

½ cup soy, coconut, cashew, or other milk

In a saucepan, simmer ingredients over low heat, stirring for a few minutes.

Allow to cool very slightly, then dredge the cake squares in this mixture on all sides, then dredge in some flaked coconut and set on parchment to cool.

You'll have to sweep up after eating these, for the crumbs of love that you offer me are the crumbs I've left behind.

LEAVE ME ALONE

mushy peas
DON'T LOOK AT ME.

MUSHY PEAS

1 package frozen green peas (about 10 to 12 ounces; you CAN also use fresh)
About 1/3 cup cashew or other milk or broth (or combo)
Salt and pepper, to taste
A little parsley or other herb
½ teaspoon lemon juice
2 or 3 tablespoons oil

Cook peas for several minutes in a little water. If using fresh, it might take a bit longer. Drain and put in a food processor with half of the oil and the other ingredients (or mash).

Return to pan with the oil and cook for a few more minutes while stirring, adjusting seasoning to taste. Have it as is or spice it up with apple, plum, and a brand new pear.

RAISE THE BOWL
PHO

PHO

Toast and then crush/break these spices:

3 star anise

2 bay leaves

1 piece lemongrass (about 2 inches)

12 cloves

1 teaspoon coriander berries

1 piece cinnamon (about 2 inches)

2 or 3 black cardamom pods

1 teaspoon fennel seed

Roast these:

1 head garlic (then peel)

1 split onion, peeled

2 carrots

1 jalapeño, split

1 piece ginger (about 2 inches)

Add also:

1 teaspoon toasted rice powder

Slice the roasted ginger and carrots, and split the onion halves again. Bring all of the above ingredients to boil with 8 cups water, 1 teaspoon salt (more to taste), and ½ teaspoon black pepper in a stock pot, and then lower to simmer. Cook for about an hour.

You can add some kitchen bouquet or tamari to this too for a fuller flavor, and a tablespoon or two of oil to attempt a little fatty burbles. You'll want it to cook down a bit I'm not tryin' to get stuck in this brine so don't turn on ya waterworks.

While that's happening, prep:
A batch rice noodles (cook them and drain)
Basil, cilantro, and limes, chopped
Some mung bean sprouts, rinsed
Some carrots, grated or ribboned
Scallion, chopped
Jalapeño or two/Thai chilies, sliced
Hoisin, sriracha, or sambal, have on hand
Set all of that aside.

Adjust broth seasonings to taste. Cut up either tofu, tempeh, fake meat, mushrooms, or eggplant, and sauté in oil, adding tamari and garlic, until browned.

Strain broth and return to heat. Add the tofu, a sliced onion, and a little more chopped carrot, and minced garlic and ginger. Red and green bell pepper strips are also nice. Simmer for 10 more minutes.

Place some noodles in each bowl. Add some tofu and cooked vegetables using a slotted spoon. Ladle broth over the top to just cover. Embellish with your accouterments.

Kylie
pop tarte

POP TARTE

A roll of puff pastry
A little oil
½ cup cocoa powder
2 or 3 tablespoons soy or other milk
$^{1}/_{3}$ cup powdered sugar + several tablespoons
$^{1}/_{3}$ cup marmalade or favorite jam

Mix cocoa powder and $^{1}/_{3}$ cup powdered sugar together. Add "milk" slowly to make a thick paste. Chill. Then mix jam with several tablespoons of powdered sugar so the world appears this day so sweet. Chill.

This is easy: Unfold the puff pastry and cut into 6 or 9 squares (it will probably be folded in thirds in the package). Slice each square via the thickness (knife blade parallel to cutting board, you see), leaving a bit of a seam on the left side attached so that you can open the square like a book. If that's confusing, use your head: You're going to fill each square and reseal it, so come to the logical conclusion about how to cut it given this information, okay!?

Spread some of the cocoa mixture on one half and some of the jam mixture on the other half. Fold the pastry back together and crimp the edges.

Bake on lightly greased or parchment-lined baking sheet at 425 degrees for 12 to 20 minutes, or until browned.

There's your pop tarte! Do not put these in the toaster.

ranch
dressing
THE SANDMAN'S MUD

RANCH DRESSING

½ cup tofu, cooked white beans, or cooked and peeled white potatoes, or a combination
1 tablespoon cider vinegar (more if needed)
½ to 1 cup fave vegan milk (no sweetener at all please!), as needed
2 tablespoons oil
Salt and white pepper, to taste
2 tablespoons carrot, chopped
1 tablespoon chive or scallion, chopped
1 tablespoon parsley, chopped
2 tablespoons onion, chopped
2 teaspoons nutritional yeast
1 peperoncino
½ to 1 teaspoon dill (either fresh or dried; if fresh, use a bit more)
¼ teaspoon ground coriander
(You could use a little white miso or tahini in this to make it more interesting.)

Begin in a food processor or blender with all ingredients except oil and milk. Add in milk in a stream until desired consistency is basically reached. Then add oil in a stream for about 20 seconds until blended and turn it off. Adjust seasonings to taste.

This is a very popular dressing: It's wanted in Galveston, it's wanted in El Dorado. This wanted dressing's in great demand.

RELEASE THE RATS
RATATOUILLE

RATATOUILLE

3 or 4 garlic cloves, minced
2 onions, diced
2 cups zucchini, sliced
1 eggplant, diced
2 cups green and red bell peppers, diced
2 cups tomato sauce
1 teaspoon marjoram
1 bay leaf
1 teaspoon thyme
½ teaspoon fennel seeds, crushed
½ teaspoon coriander berries, crushed
¼ cup red wine
Several tablespoons olive oil
½ cup broth
Salt and pepper, to taste
A few basil leaves

Saute onions and garlic in 2 tablespoons of olive oil for 2 minutes. Add fennel, bay leaf, and coriander and sauté for 2 more minutes. Remove from heat.

Next, sauté the other vegetables in a little oil with some salt and pepper. After 3 minutes, add the thyme and marjoram. Stir. Remove from heat.

Mix wine, broth, and tomato sauce with a little salt and pepper—such a rich, delicious sauce that I have heard and has been poured into my human heart, and filled me with love, up to the brim, and killed me. Can be improved with a little kitchen bouquet or vegan Worcestershire.

In a casserole or Dutch oven, layer the vegetables, sauce, and onions/garlic, each twice. Cover with a little sauce. Top with basil leaves. Put cover on and bake for 35 minutes at 350 degrees. Remove lid and bake for another 10 to 15 minutes.

TATOU

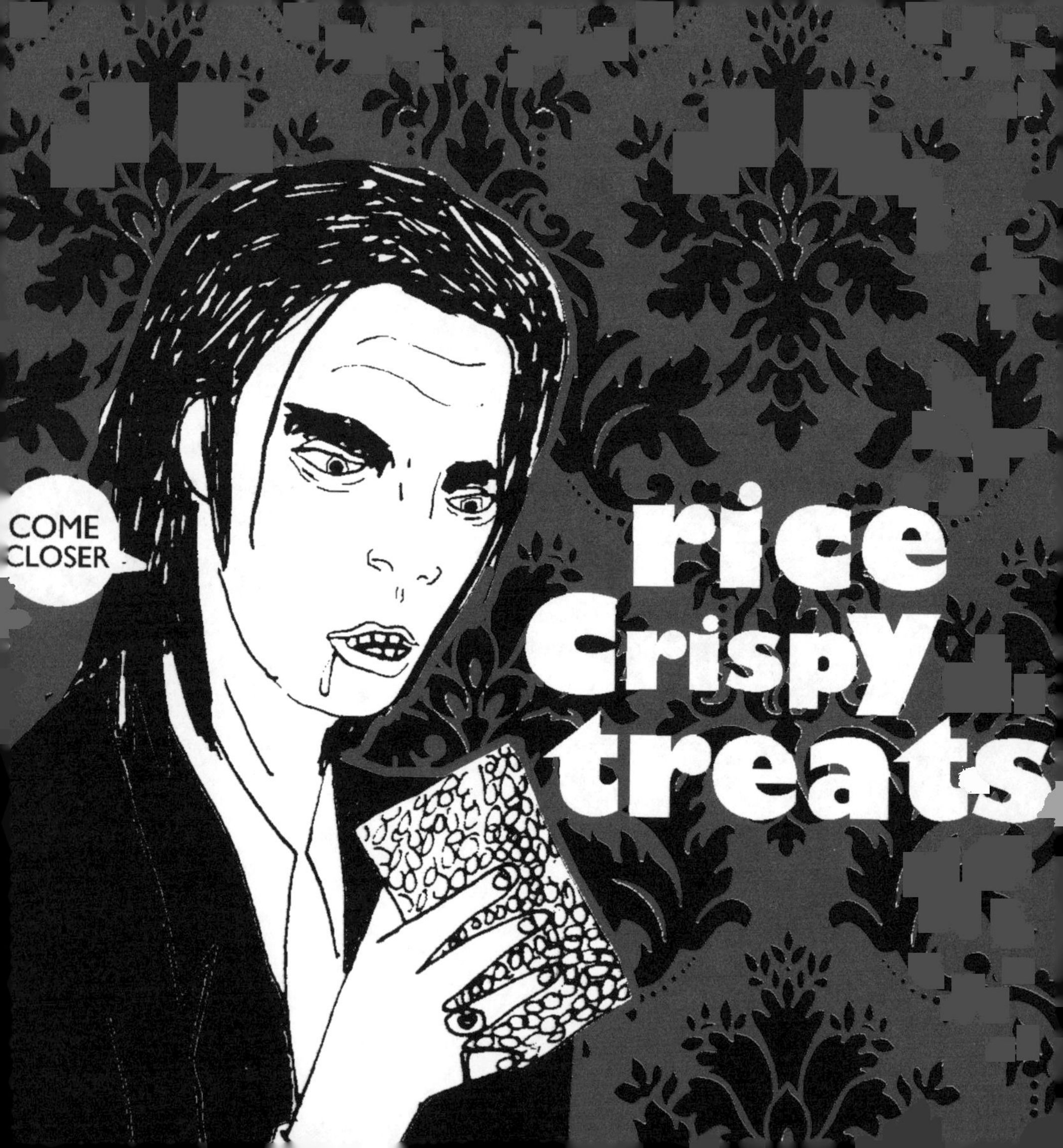
COME CLOSER
rice Crispy treats

CRISPY RICE TREATS

4 cups Rice Krispies
3 tablespoons margarine or coconut oil
2 cups vegan marshmallows
2 or 3 tablespoons of your favorite nut butter

Melt the margarine/oil. Stir in marshmallows and melt them too. Remove from heat and mix with the rest. Spread in a pan and allow to cool at room temp. And you're all done, and done is the missing, now all that remains is to sail forever upon the stain.

Chill if you wish. You can add chocolate chips, nuts, candy pieces, or whatever to this. Just don't add them when it's super hot. You can omit the nut butter, of course, if yo ass is allergic.

a reuben

REUBEN

Rye bread *(preferably swirled, which you can find where wet-lipped women with greasy fists crawled the ceilings and the walls, or at a deli or supermarket)*
Veggie meat slices
Sauerkraut
Oil, salt, and pepper

For Russian dressing:
1 tablespoon prepared horseradish (more to taste)
1 tablespoon red wine vinegar (more to taste)
¼ cup silken tofu
2 tablespoons ketchup
2 tablespoons pickle, chopped
1 garlic clove, peeled
2 tablespoons onion, grated
2 tablespoons pimientos, chopped
Chives
½ teaspoon red curry powder
¼ teaspoon dill
Salt, as you like

For Swiss sauce:
¼ cup white beans, cooked
¼ cup potato, cooked
¼ cup oil

½ cup soy milk or whatever
1 tablespoon mustard
1 tablespoon white miso
½ teaspoon agar flakes or carageenan
Salt, to taste
1 garlic clove, minced
¼ teaspoon coriander powder
¼ teaspoon white pepper
1 tablespoon white wine vinegar

Blend ingredients for Russian dressing, adjust taste, and set aside. Fry up that lunch meat, and the sauerkraut separately, and keep those warm.

Blend the cheez sauce ingredients, then heat them in a saucepan until bubbling. If too thick, add more soy milk or whatever. Adjust seasonings to taste and remove from heat.

Heat the bread slices but don't over toast them. Some people don't toast it at all, but warming it is good.

Now put it all together.

Makes a bunch of sandwiches.

AHH

SATISFY ME

SNACKERS BAR

For chocolate:

14 ounces semisweet chocolate chips
2 ounces cooking paraffin (a.k.a. canning paraffin)
2 tablespoons coconut milk
For peanutty caramel part:
1 cup roasted peanuts
1 ¼ cup brown sugar
½ cup corn syrup
1 cup vanilla vegan creamer or coconut milk
½ cup oil/margarine/coconut oil
A little salt (like ¼ teaspoon, maybe a little more)

For nougat:

1 ½ cups sugar
1 tablespoon cornstarch
1 teaspoon cream of tartar
1 teaspoon agar flakes
½ cup water
1 teaspoon vanilla
1 cup corn syrup

Mix your nougat stuff except vanilla and bring to a boil over medium heat, stirring (use a wooden spoon). Stir less frequently once sugar dissolves. Do your best to keep sugar from crystallizing on the sides of the pan—just keep pushing it back in there.

270 degrees is soft crack stage: Once it reaches this temperature, you can pour it into a lightly greased or lined square pan, and allow to cool. Cut into pieces and chill (think candy-bar-shaped pieces).

Caramel is next. Melt sugar and oil in a pan with corn syrup. After it starts bubbling, add creamer, then add peanuts. Again, you're going to want to avoid crystallization as mentioned earlier. Once it begins to thicken nicely remove from heat and pour into a heat resistant bowl. 244 degrees is your temperature for this one, soft ball. Cool and then chill.

Slowly melt paraffin in a double boiler. It will take some time, and yes, it's flammable, so you want to not heat it too quickly, though I said before I'd pay for all the damages.[1] Once it's melted add chocolate and coconut milk until they've melted, blending thoroughly.

1 for entertainment purposes only, will not pay for any damages

Take strips of the nougat, top with some peanut caramel then drizzle chocolate over to cover. Allow to firm up/cool a bit, then turn them and do the bottom. Chill.

Use your wiles to keep these bar shaped and to not burn yourself.

Needless to say, this is not the same paraffin as the one made out of coal or petroleum. It is made out of vegetable or other edible oils.

I'M SO...
HAPPY
spaghetti
and
rice balls

SPAGHETTI AND RICE BALLS

You need spaghetti sauce:

4 cups tomatoes, seeded
1 onion, diced
1 green bell pepper, diced
1 red bell pepper, diced
1 carrot, grated
1 teaspoon oregano, minced
3 garlic cloves, minced
Salt, pepper, and red pepper flakes to taste
2 tablespoons olive oil
½ cup mushroom broth (more if needed)

For balls:

1 cup mushrooms, chopped
1 ½ cup rice, cooked
¼ cup potato starch
1 teaspoon garlic powder
1 tablespoon oil + some for frying
2 tablespoons onion, grated
½ teaspoon cumin
2 tablespoons tamari
1 teaspoon smoked paprika
Salt, to taste
¼ cup Italian parsley, minced

Cook the tomato sauce ingredients for 20 minutes. Allow to cool a bit. Puree and then bring up to heat again and simmer for 10 minutes, adjusting seasoning to taste.

Mush all of the ingredients for balls together, and then make them into smallish balls. Fry in light oil, turning, until something's gotten hold of your hand dragging your soul to a beautiful land, and browned all over and set aside on absorbent paper.

Cook your spaghetti until something has invaded your nights, painting your sleep with a color so bright, and al dente. Drain.

Put this all together as you see fit.

WHOAHH
Stuffed
MUSHROOMS

STUFFED MUSHROOMS

20 big button/crimini mushrooms, take the stems out (you can use some of them in the filling!)
1 cup pecans, chopped (more maybe, you can also do half or all hazelnuts)
½ cup flat-leafed parsley
½ cup basil (fresh, duh)
5 cloves garlic
¼ cup onion, chopped
1 to 2 tablespoons lemon juice
2 tablespoons nutritional yeast
Chili flakes, to taste
Salt and pepper, to taste
A little sage
A little oil is a great idea or use some nut milk
Some parsley to garnish

Blend half of the pecans with the other ingredients except mushrooms. Mix in the rest of the pecans, adjusting flavors, and stuff the mushroom caps with this business.

Place in baking dish and broil for 4 to 5 minutes, and remember that to escape the stench of human corruption into an oven they did crawl.

Garnish with parsley.

A TOFU DOG
WOOF

TOFU DOG

8 buns
½ cup sauerkraut
4 tablespoons brown mustard
4 long pickle spears
1 onion, sliced
1 block extra firm tofu
Black pepper, to taste
2 tablespoons vegan Worcestershire sauce
½ teaspoon liquid smoke
1 teaspoon smoked paprika
1 ½ teaspoons turmeric
1 cup favorite broth or tomato/ vegetable juice
Salt, to taste
Oil, to sauté

Cut tofu block in half, face-wise (maximize surface area). Press the water out by placing in paper towels and setting a baking sheet on top with a pot full of water on top of that for about 30 minutes.

Cut each half into 4 long strips. In baking dish, soak in black pepper, Worcestershire, smoke, broth, salt to taste, spices, and about 2 tablespoons of oil. Allow to sit for an hour, turning once. Then bake at 325 degrees for an hour. Remove them from liquid when ready.

Sauté onions in a little oil with some salt and pepper until browned. Do the same with sauerkraut.

Toast the buns. Put the hot dogs under the broiler for 3 minutes a side (on some sort of pan, you scallywag!!). Take a dog. Then you hold it so carelessly close, tell it it's dirty. Place in bun.

One dog per bun, with mustard, pickle, fried sauerkraut and fried onions. Maybe some vegan mayo on there. Personally I like arugula on it as well.

veggie
meatloaf
BE
MINE

VEGGIE MEATLOAF

2 cups soy protein (rehydrated) or cooked quinoa
1 block firm tofu, crumbled, or 2 cups beans, cooked and mashed
2 cups lentils, cooked
1 cup potato starch
¼ cup tamari (more to taste)
½ cup tomato paste
1 cup peas, cooked
1 cup carrots, diced
1 cup onion, diced
1 bell pepper, diced
1 tablespoon mixed dried herbs
1 teaspoon ground cumin
1 teaspoon paprika
1 cup broth

Mix all together, pour into lightly greased large loaf pan or other baking dish.

Bake at 375 degrees for 40 minutes or until done to your liking. You can cover with foil for part of the cooking time, if you like. You can also let it sit overnight in the fridge and then cook it the next day. Oh, and yesterday is gone forever and ever, never to be again.

Personally, I like this served with a sauce that is half my favorite gravy, and half tomato sauce with a little tamarind in it.

veggie
pot pie
NOMGG

VEGGIE POT PIE

2 not-sweet 9-inch pie crusts
1 cup potatoes, diced small
1 cup broccoli, chopped
1 cup cauliflower, chopped
1 cup mushrooms, chopped
1 carrot, diced
1 onion, diced
1 cup peas
2 garlic cloves, minced
¼ cup flour
1 ½ cups broth
2 tablespoons nutritional yeast
1 teaspoon sage, crushed
Black or white pepper and salt, to taste
1 teaspoon curry powder or turmeric

Roll out the pie crust, place one in a lightly greased 9-inch pie pan. Mix the other things together and season to taste. Cover with the other pie crust. Crimp the edges, of course. Poke a few times with a fork.

Bake at 425 degrees for 15 minutes, then lower heat to 375 and bake for another 30 minutes.

Though the carnival is over, you will love this til you die.

Adieu.